The WISDOM EXPRESS

Published by Mindstir Media, LLC
45 Lafayette Rd | Suite 181| North Hampton, NH 03862 | USA
1.800.767.0531 | www.mindstirmedia.com

Printed in the United States of America
ISBN-13: 978-1-7368410-6-8

The WISDOM EXPRESS

Jeff Wineinger

MINDSTIR MEDIA

This book is dedicated to Wyllieanne
because they are my family and I love them.

LISTEN AND LEARN

Listen to God

And look for His working,

For behind every happening His instruction is lurking.

Some events will appear to make zero sense,

And others even less-

But when meaning is revealed and instruction unsealed

We see that our lives He did bless!

PURPOSE OF THIS BOOK

The purpose of this book is not only for instruction to improve one's life, but also to introduce the reader to a person.

JESUS IS THAT PERSON.

For the preaching of the cross is to them that perish foolishness; but unto us which are saved it is the power of God.
1 Co 1:18

GOD SEES EVERYTHING

Proverbs 15:3 The eyes of the Lord are in every place,
beholding the evil and the good.

God's eyes are everywhere,
If you want to hide,
That might not seem fair.
But He watches closely because He loves us much-
Even if you hurt your knee and need a crutch.
Floating in the ocean with no land in sight
He sees you during the darkest night.
Don't worry because He knows you're there
And this is the greatest type of care.

KIND WORDS

Proverbs 15:1 A soft answer turneth away wrath (anger): but grevious words stir up anger.

God says there's a way we ought to talk,
It's not with a ferocious roar or squawk.
Rather, when someone speaks in an angry way,
A kind reply might brighten their day.
Speaking nice when someone is mean
Can often be a difficult thing.
But yelling back won't help at all,
And any hope for peace will fall.
A kind reply from a gentle hare
Can soothe the wrath of an angry bear.

GOSSIP

Proverbs 26:22 The words of a talebearer are as wounds, they go down into the innermost parts of the belly.

A talebearer and a gossip are one-in-the-same,
They talk about others and it's a shame.
For gossip hurts down deep in your heart,
And can pull the closest of friends apart.
Whether what's being said is a lie or even true,
God is serious that it's something we shouldn't do.
If gossip starts when you are there,
Don't join in or try to share-
Simply change the talk, or leave on a walk.
That's what these horses should have done
rather than whispering about Donkey for fun.

EVERYTHING HAS A PURPOSE

Proverbs 21:31 The horse is prepared against the day of battle: but safety is of the Lord.

There's a purpose for every event-
A reason for all that is,
Even getting a flat tire or passing your quiz.
God has a plan for your life
Just let Him take lead,
There will be joy and strife
But a lesson, so take heed.
With God in control there's no luck or chance,
Whether getting a new toy or a tear in your pants!
But it's comforting to know
That God planned it all for you to grow.

REPUTATION

Proverbs 20:11 Even a child is known by his doings, whether his work be pure, and whether it be right.

It doesn't matter whatever your age,

Whether newly born or wise old sage.

The way we act and behave is a clue,

Telling others we're good, or belong in a zoo.

If we're known as pure and right,

God says that's out of sight.

So what? Who cares? What's the big deal? you may ask-

Regarding how I do my task.

Well, a person can be mean, rude or gentle as a dove,

But as a Christian our actions are to show God's love.

Our simple deeds like holding open a door

Show the kindness of Jesus at the grocery store.

DON'T MAKE EXCUSES

Proverbs 23:13 The slothful (lazy) man saith, There is a lion without (outside), I shall be slain in the streets.

What needs to be done
Is the thing we should do,
Not being lazy or crying boo-hoo!
When a task is boring, hard or both-
Finishing it quickly will lead to growth.
Some folks will whine, complain and even fuss,
Over such simple things as waking early for the bus.
Not making excuses is best God said,
Whether it's doing dishes
Or brushing your teeth before bed!

HOLD YOUR TONGUE

Proverbs 17:28 Even a fool, when he holdeth his peace (keeps quiet), is counted wise: and he that shutteth his lips (doesn't talk) is esteemed a man of understanding.

Holding your tongue means not to talk,

For some this would be quite a shock.

The Bible says too much jibber-jabber, blabber and blubble-

Will not be good and lead to trouble.

But if one's not smart, or even a fool-

By keeping quiet they'll appear a jewel.

There are some folks who truly are wise-

They use few words and watch with their eyes.

A turkey is not the brightest of fowls,

But holding its gobble will impress these owls!

CHOOSE GOOD FRIENDS

Proverbs 13:20 He that walketh with wise men shall be wise; but a companion of fools shall be destroyed.

In this life there's no greater joy
Than a friend who'll share their brand new toy.
Friends help us when we're sad,
And honest if our dance move is bad.
But this business of friendship is no small deal,
To God, it's importance is quite real.
Friends guide us to good choices or not-
Like being big helpers or thieves that get caught.
If you were a fish and had to decide,
Would you play ball, or bite toes in the tide?

THE POWER OF THE TONGUE

Proverbs 18:21 Death and life are in the power of the tongue: and they that love it shall eat the fruit thereof.

There's a member in your head,

That we wiggle when something's to be said.

You poke it out of your mouth when you tease,

But must keep it in while chewing your peas.

This thing is our tongue-or words we say,

And is able to make armies fight or stay.

Words come from the heart, which is a great place to start.

Jesus will make it new, custom tailored just for you.

The Bible tells us our tongue cannot be tamed,

And without God it will make us ashamed.

But with His help it's possible of course,

Even if it's wild as a horse.

INSTRUCTION AND CORRECTION
ARE PART OF LIFE

Proverbs 6:23 For the commandment is a lamp; and the law is light; and reproofs (corrections) of instruction are the way of life...

God's instructions are pure and true,

He always knows what's best for you.

But sometimes our choices are not clear,

So we pray that our lives He will steer.

Yet still sometimes we trip and stumble,

Which may simply be Him keeping us humble.

But knowing now that He'll teach us each day,

It's clearly important to listen and pray.

Correction and instruction will help this worm,

So when birds fly near it won't have to squirm.

WORK BEFORE PLAY

Proverbs 24:27 Prepare thy work without, and make it fit for thyself in the field; and afterwards build thine house.

When it comes to the order of work and play,
We'd better check what God has to say.
Proverbs tells us chores first and then play,
This is best and not the other way.
Often it's hard when the game is fun,
But it's better when your work's already done.
If we did no work and only play-
Think of the horses who'd have no hay.
If there were no builders,
We'd have no park or slide,
Or bicycle for Octopus to ride.

BE SLOW TO ANGER

Proverbs 14:29 He that is slow to wrath (anger) is of great understanding; but he that is hasty of spirit exalteth folly.

When things we want don't seem to go right,
It's quite easy to throw a fit all night.
But losing one's temper at the drop of a hat-
is actually a sin, if you can imagine that!
Being upset and angry is natural you see-
But first consider Jesus and if He'd agree.
Understanding God's patience and love
May stop us from giving a shove.
And by this our actions will make Him glad,
By knowing when and when not to get mad.
If our ringmaster's strict but the circus is our job-
Should we juggle, or squish him to a blob?

TOO MUCH OF A GOOD THING

Proverbs 25:16 Hast thou found honey? Eat so much as is sufficient (or a good amount) for thee, lest thou be filled therewith, and vomit it.

According to God there is a rule,

Of how much to have without being a fool.

Some items are sweet, salty or funny-

But one can have too much, even of honey.

This proverb teaches it's not just about food,

Even talking because too much is rude.

Or maybe it's our playtime we don't want to stop,

But too much of this may cause our grades to drop.

So in the end we see there are measures,

Even a limit for Snail's tasty treasures.

THINK OF GOD IN ALL YOU DO

*Proverbs 4:26 Ponder the path of they feet
and let all thy ways be established.*

To ponder our path means to think-
Do our choices please God, or do they stink?
Pause and reflect for a spell-
Is there anything we do
That we'd rather not tell?
This question's answer will help us plan,
Ask God for help, because of course He can!
Often God's lead we can't hear or feel,
Sometimes He's gentle or hard as steel.
We only need our heart to seek Him,
Having no fear we're out on a limb.
When God's in your heart you'll help the poor,
And love telling others of Jesus more.

Am I quick to
help the poor?

Am I loving and tell
others about Jesus?

14

CPSIA information can be obtained
at www.ICGtesting.com
Printed in the USA
BVHW021216160521
607357BV00015B/257